<small>STEP-BY-STEP</small>
50 Perfect Pasta Dishes

STEP-BY-STEP

50 Perfect Pasta Dishes

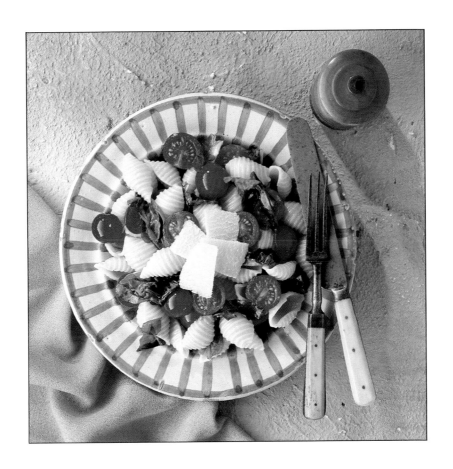

Maxine Clark

Photography by Edward Allwright

ACROPOLIS BOOKS

First published in 1994 by Lorenz Books

© Anness Publishing Limited 1994

Lorenz Books is an imprint of
Anness Publishing Limited
1 Boundary Row
London SE1 8HP

Reprinted in 1995, 1996.

ISBN 1 85967 001 6

A CIP catalogue record is available from the British Library

Publisher: Joanna Lorenz
Series Editor: Lindsay Porter
Assistant Editor: Charles Moxham
Designers: Peter Butler, Peter Laws
Home Economist: Jenny Shapter
Photographer: Edward Allwright
Stylist: Hilary Guy

Typeset by MC Typeset Ltd, Rochester, Kent
Printed and bound in Hong Kong

CONTENTS

INTRODUCTION

Pasta has rapidly become one of today's staple foods, travelling across the world in various forms as far as Asia and South America. Its origins are unclear, but a type of pasta was certainly made in Sicily, the 'grain store' of Rome, in the days of the Roman Empire. It has also existed in China and Japan for many centuries, but in very different forms and shapes.

The enormous popularity of pasta is due to its incredible versatility, and its value for money. Pasta can stretch a few store-cupboard ingredients to make a satisfying meal fit for a king! You can produce sauces with small amounts of meat, mix them with pasta and produce a filling and nutritious dish. Most wheat-flour-and-water (commercial dried) pasta contains more proteins and carbohydrates than potatoes, so when combined with a sauce of vegetables, cheese or meat, it gives a good nutritional balance. It is a fine source of energy too – better than sugar, as it releases energy at a slower prolonged rate, and will give you a lift if you are tired and hungry. Pasta is only fattening if eaten in over-large quantities with too much sauce! Italians fill up on the pasta itself, the sauce being an adornment to enhance the flavour.

Pasta is very easy to make at home if you have patience and a little time to spare. The result is exciting and delicious, even if it is a little soggy to begin with! It's a little like making bread: once you have mastered the technique, you can make one of life's staples. Fresh egg pasta is made *only* with wheat flour, eggs, a little salt and olive oil. Do not be tempted to add water as it will toughen the pasta and make it sticky. The main thing is to enjoy the process and the results *con gusto*.

Pasta Types

When buying dried pasta, choose good-quality well-known brands. Of the 'fresh' pasta sold in sealed packs in supermarkets, the filled or stuffed varieties are worth buying; noodles and ribbon pasta are better bought dried, as these tend to have more bite when cooked. However, if you are lucky enough to live near an Italian delicatessen where pasta is made on the premises, it will usually be of very good quality. Fresh is not necessarily better, but the final choice is yours – the best pasta is home-made, as then you can be sure of the quality of the ingredients used and also of the finished texture.

You will see from this book that the sauces are almost limitless in their variety, as are the pasta shapes themselves. There are no hard-and-fast rules regarding which shape to use with which pasta sauce: it's really a matter of personal preference. However, there are a few guidelines to follow, such as that thin spaghetti suits seafood sauces, thicker spaghetti is good with creamy sauces (as in, for instance, Spaghetti alla Carbonara) and thick tubular pasta, like rigatoni, penne and so on, suits rustic sauces full of bits that will be caught in the pasta itself.

macaroni

vermicelli

quick-cook macaroni

fresh cuttlefish-ink tagliatelle

orzo or puntalette

small soup pasta

tagliatelle: tomato, spinach and plain

fresh caramellone

fettuccia ricc

fresh ravioli

fresh cappelletti

lasagne lur

fresh tortelloni

garg

'paglia e fieno' ('straw and hay' tagliarini)

spaghetti

spinach spaghetti

papperdelle

*fresh beetroot
tagliatelle*

*fresh wild-mushroom
tagliatelle*

wholemeal (wholewheat) spaghetti

pipe rigate

*conchigliette rigate
(small soup pasta shells)*

pasta bows (farfalle)

campanelle

cannelloni

rigatoni

pasta shells (conchiglie)

spirali

lasagne

spinach lasagne

wholemeal (wholewheat) shells

orecchite

Herbs and Spices

Both fresh and dried herbs can be used successfully to enhance the flavour of most pasta sauces. Certain herbs have an affinity with particular ingredients, and are added to bring out their flavours or to accentuate them. Tomatoes are the natural sauce ingredient, and their taste can be changed completely by the incorporation of different herbs and spices. Fresh herbs, although expensive in supermarkets, are a must for a sauce like pesto. Dried basil has none of the Mediterranean pungency needed in this wonderfully evocative sauce. The colour of fresh herbs brings a visual charm to sauces, as well as adding a truly fresh flavour. Buy growing herbs in pots and – despite instructions to the contrary on the packaging – try planting them out in the garden in summer or, as I do, in a windowbox. They will grow in a sunny, well-drained spot if cut regularly (but not too much). Stating that they cannot be planted out is a commercial ploy to make you buy more.

Ideally use fresh herbs immediately after cutting, but if you have to keep them for any length of time, most will store well in a jar of water covered with a sealed polythene bag and placed in the refrigerator.

Dried herbs are very useful if they are not too old. Freeze-dried are the best as they retain both colour and flavour. Use half the quantity of dried herbs as you would fresh, for the flavour is more concentrated. Store dried herbs in air-tight containers, in a dark dry cupboard.

Basil
Fresh basil is *the* herb for pasta dishes, and dried basil is a poor substitute. If fresh basil is unavailable, use a spoonful of ready-made pesto sauce instead of the dried herb for a better taste. The flavour is a pungent mixture of cinnamon and anise: it is too difficult to describe, so just find some and use it – the more, the better! Basil is wonderful with tomatoes and in delicate ricotta cheese fillings. It is lost, however, in hearty meaty sauces.

Bay leaves
Bay is often used to enhance the flavour of meat sauces and to give a delicate flavour to béchamel or white sauces.

Dill (dillweed)
A herb with a slightly aniseed flavour which marries well with fish, especially fresh or smoked salmon.

Garlic
Used in moderation, garlic is a marvellous flavour enhancer. However, the longer you cook it, the more mellow the flavour. It is good in most dishes where a strong onion taste is required – meat sauces, anything with tomato, and with pulses and beans. Choose big fat cloves for a fuller, less bitter flavour.

Oregano and marjoram
Oregano and marjoram are the most popular herbs used in Italy, along with basil and sage. They have an affinity with tomatoes and eggs, and make a pretty garnish when in flower. Oregano is a wilder strain and more astringent than marjoram, which has a sweeter flavour.

Parsley (curly and flat-leaf)
Parsley is a very versatile herb and both types of parsley impart a fresh 'green' flavour to almost any dish. The common curly variety is good for chopping and the pretty flat-leafed one is lovely roughly chopped or used as a leafy garnish. A delicious pesto sauce can be made using parsley instead of basil.

Rocket (arugula)
Rocket, with its slightly peppery taste, can be used both as a herb and, more commonly, as a salad ingredient. In this book it is simply stirred into a pasta dish at the end of cooking so that it wilts like spinach, but is still crunchy.

Sage
A classic Italian herb available in many varieties. It has a lovely earthy flavour and is good with meat and some cheeses such as Gorgonzola.

Chillies (dried and fresh)
Use smaller quantities of dried chillies than fresh – they add heat and spiciness to sauces such as arrabbiata. Wear rubber gloves when preparing fresh chillies, or work under running water, and don't rub your eyes as the juice of both dried and fresh chillies can be painful. Green or red chillies can be used – the quantities are variable depending on your taste, but to be on the safe side add less than specified in the recipe: you can always add more.

Nutmeg
The kernel of a nut that also produces mace, nutmeg gives a rich musky flavour to white sauces and is good with cheese.

Saffron
These orange filaments are the stigma of the saffron crocus, one of the world's most expensive spices, but a little goes a long way. Saffron is also available in powdered form. This delicate spice will impart a wonderful aroma and colour to any dish.

dried chillies

bay

saffron

rocket (arugula)

oregano

dill (dillweed)

fresh chillies

garlic

basil

sage

nutmeg

purple marjoram

curly parsley

flat-leaf parsley

Sauces and Pastes

There is an infinite variety of ready-made sauces and pastes available which you can add to your own sauce to make it richer or to deepen the flavour. Some can even be incorporated into pasta dough: for example, you can make mushroom or tomato or even pesto pasta.

Anchovies: salted

Whole anchovies preserved in salt which need to be rinsed and the backbone removed before use. They have a a fresher flavour than canned anchovy fillets in oil. Used in moderation, anchovies add a fishy depth to sauces and soups.

Capers

These are little green flower buds picked before they open and preserved in vinegar or salt. They add a sharp piquancy to rich sauces and are particularly good with tomatoes and cheese.

Carbonara sauce

Although your own version made from the recipe in this book will be much better, ready-made carbonara sauce is a useful standby for a quick meal – add sautéed fresh mushrooms or more bacon to make it go further.

Garlic: chopped

A great time-saver, eliminating the need for peeling and chopping. Use it straight out of the jar.

Mushroom paste

A delicacy available from Italian delicatessens. Add a generous spoonful to freshly cooked pasta with a little cream for a quick sauce, or to pasta dough to make mushroom pasta.

Olive paste

Cuts out all that stoning (pitting) and chopping. Delicious stirred into hot pasta with chopped fresh tomato or added by the spoonful to enrich a tomato or meat sauce.

Pesto

The commercial version of fresh basil pesto. Brands vary, but it is a very useful store-cupboard standby to stir into hot pasta and soups.

Pesto: fresh

Some supermarkets produce their own 'fresh' pesto, sold in tubs in the chilled cabinet. This is infinitely superior to the bottled variety, although your own freshly made pesto will be even better.

Pesto: red

A commercial sauce made from tomatoes and red peppers to stir into hot pasta or soups.

Tomato pasta sauce

Again, a good standby or base for a quick meal. Vary by adding chopped anchovies and olives, or pour over freshly cooked stuffed pasta.

Tomato purée (paste)

An essential if you are making a sauce from insipid fresh tomatoes! It will intensify any tomato-based sauce and will help thicken meat sauces. It will also make tomato pasta if added to the basic ingredients.

Tomatoes: canned plum

No store-cupboard should be without these – invaluable for making any tomato sauce or stew when good fresh tomatoes are not available.

Tomatoes: canned chopped

Usually made from Italian plum tomatoes which have a fuller flavour than most, these are the heart of a good tomato sauce if you cannot find really ripe red tasty fresh tomatoes.

Tomatoes: passata

A useful store-cupboard ingredient, this is pulped tomato that has been strained to remove the seeds. It makes a good base for a tomato sauce, though chopped canned tomatoes can also be used.

Tomatoes: sun-dried in oil

These tomatoes are drained and chopped and added to tomato-based dishes to give a deeper, almost roasted tomato flavour.

Left: *There are many ready-prepared sauces and pastes available. From top left: passata, salted anchovies, mushroom paste, olive paste, tomato purée (paste), chopped tomato, carbonara sauce, canned plum tomatoes, capers, tomato pasta sauce, red pesto, pesto, fresh pesto, sun-dried tomatoes in oil, chopped garlic.*

Eastern Pasta

Various forms of noodle or pasta exist outside Europe. They are found mainly in China and Japan, but also throughout Malaysia, Hong Kong and the rest of the Far East, including parts of India and Tibet.

This pasta, usually in noodle form and often enhanced with a sprinkling of vegetables or fish, adds variety to the sometimes monotonous staple diet of rice and beans eaten by the poorer sections of the population. Some types of pasta are used to give bulk to soups; others are eaten as a filling dish to stave off hunger during the day. They are made from the staple crops of each region – whether rice flour, soya bean flour or potato flour – and are cooked in different ways: some are soaked and then fried, some are boiled and fried and some are rolled out and stuffed like ravioli, but most are simply boiled. Some turn transparent when cooked.

Oriental egg noodles are usually made with wheat flour and can be treated in the same way as ordinary Western pasta. Buckwheat and fresh wholemeal (wholewheat) noodles are similarly cooked. Fresh white noodles do not contain egg but are cooked in the same way as egg noodles. Some dried egg noodles come in discs or blocks and are 'cooked' by immersion in boiling water in which they are then left to soak for a few minutes. As with Western pasta, oriental noodles can be flavoured with other ingredients such as prawns (shrimp), carrot and spinach. Won-ton skins, like thin squares of rolled-out pasta, are used for stuffing and making different filled

shapes. Although oriental pasta is available in a variety of long noodle types, it doesn't seem to be made into the shapes we are used to seeing in Europe and America: you will often find it wound into balls and beautifully packaged.

Above: *Eastern noodles include (from top left, clockwise) Oriental rice flour noodles, rice vermicelli, rice stick noodles, hand-made amoy flour vermicelli, medium egg noodles, fresh brown mein, egg noodles, rice stick vermicelli, fresh thin egg noodles, Japanese wheat flour noodles, Ho Fan vermicelli, spinach vegetable noodles, carrot vegetable noodles, won ton skins, wheat flour noodles, fresh white mein, buckwheat noodles, shrimp egg noodles.*

Basic Sauce Ingredients

Clams
These tiny shellfish are used to make sauces and soups. Fresh cockles are a good substitute, as are canned clams in brine.

Dolcelatte
An Italian, blue-veined, creamy cheese used in sauces and fillings.

Feta
Feta is firm and crumbly with a salty taste from the brine in which it is preserved.

Gorgonzola
An Italian, blue-veined, semi-soft cheese with a piquant flavour. Used in sauces and stuffings.

Italian sausages
Meaty, highly seasoned fresh sausages used to make quick sauces and stuffings.

Mediterranean prawns (shrimp)
Raw or cooked, these large prawns have more flavour than smaller varieties.

Mussels
As with clams, mussels are best fresh, but frozen cooked ones can be substituted.

Olives
Used in sauces to add richness, black olives have more flavour than the green kind.

Onions
Spanish onions add sweetness and red or purple types add a mild flavour and attractive colour.

Pancetta
Italian streaky bacon sold smoked or unsmoked, sliced or in a piece, to add flavour to sauces.

Parmesan
A hard cheese for grating and serving with pasta, made from semi-skimmed unpasteurized cow's milk.

Peppers: red and yellow
Red and yellow peppers make a delicious addition to a sauce and are good with cold pasta salad.

Pine nuts
These small creamy-coloured nuts are essential in pesto.

Pistachios
Pale green nuts from the Middle East which are used in sweet and savoury dishes.

Ricotta
An Italian whey cheese which is soft and creamy. It is especially good in sweet or savoury fillings.

Smoked salmon
Cold smoked salmon can be thinly sliced and added to sauces and fillings.

Spinach
Spinach is an iron-rich, leafy, green vegetable mainly used to flavour and colour pasta dough.

Tomatoes
Choose only really ripe tomatoes – plum if possible. Miniature or cherry tomatoes make a good addition to sauces.

Walnuts
Walnuts are used in sweet and savoury dishes. They are also used in walnut pesto.

black olives

smoked salmon

pancetta

spinach

Italian sausages

feta

Parmesan

red and yellow (bell) peppers

Gorgonzola

onions

Dolcelatte

mussels

pistachios

clams

ricotta

pine nuts

pear tomatoes

plum tomato

walnuts

diterranean
wns (shrimp)

cherry tomatoes

Equipment

To make pasta, a bare minimum of equipment is needed – practised hands would say that only a clean table top and a rolling pin were necessary. However, there are several gadgets to make pasta making easier and less hard work.

Bowls
A set of bowls is useful for mixing, whisking and so on.

Chopping board
A hygienic nylon board is recommended for cutting and chopping.

Colander
A large colander is essential for draining cooked pasta quickly.

Cook's knife
A large all-purpose cook's knife is essential for cutting pasta and for chopping.

Flour dredger
Useful for dusting pasta with small amounts of flour.

Large metal spoon
For folding in and serving sauces.

Measuring spoons
For accurately measuring quantities of ingredients.

Pasta machine or roller
Vital for kneading, rolling and cutting pasta – a real labour-saver. Attachments for other shapes are available.

Pasta or pastry wheel
For cutting pasta with a decorated edge, such as pasta bows.

Pastry brush
For removing excess flour from pasta and for brushing pasta with water, milk or beaten egg to seal.

Perforated spoon
Useful for draining small amounts of food.

Pestle and mortar
For hand-grinding pesto and crushing black peppercorns.

Ravioli cutter
For cutting or stamping out individual raviolis; can be round or square. A selection of pastry cutters will serve the same purpose.

Ravioli tray (raviolatore)
For making sheets of ravioli quickly and neatly – with practice!

Rolling pin
Pasta pins are available in specialist shops. These are long, thin and tapered at each end, but you have to be quite adept to use them. An ordinary heavy wooden rolling pin will do.

Small grater
For freshly grating nutmeg and Parmesan cheese.

Vegetable knife
For preparing vegetables and paring lemons, and for delicate work.

Vegetable peeler (parer)
For shaving Parmesan cheese and chocolate.

Whisk
Essential for beating eggs thoroughly and combining sauces smoothly.

bowls

pasta machine

cook's knife

measuring spoons

flour dredger

rolling pin

pestle and mortar

cutters

colander

large metal spoon

perforated spoon

chopping board

vegetable knife

pastry brush

metal whisk

vegetable peeler

pastry wheel

small grater

ravioli cutter

ravioli tray

To Cook Pasta

1 Throw the pasta into a large pan of boiling salted water. Stir once to prevent sticking. The addition of 15 ml/1 tbsp vegetable or olive oil will help to stop the water boiling over and prevent the pasta from sticking. *Do not cover* or the water will boil over.

2 Quickly bring the pasta back to a rolling boil and boil until *al dente* (literally 'to the tooth') – the pasta should be just firm to the bite. It should not have a hard centre or be very floppy.

3 Quickly drain the pasta well, using a large colander or sieve (strainer). Immediately rinse the pasta with boiling water to wash off any starch and to prevent the pasta from sticking together. At this stage you can toss the pasta in a little olive oil or butter if not dressing with the sauce immediately. Serve hot pasta straight away. It is up to you whether you toss the pasta with the sauce before serving or serve it with the sauce on top.

COOKING TIMES FOR FRESH AND DRIED PASTA

Calculate the cooking time from the moment the water returns to the boil after the pasta has been added.

Unfilled pasta
Fresh: 2–3 minutes, though some very thin pasta is ready as soon as the water returns to the boil.
Dried: 8–12 minutes, but keep checking as this is only a guide.

Filled pasta
Fresh: 8–10 minutes.
Dried: 15–20 minutes.

Basic Pasta Dough

Allow 200 g/7 oz/1¾ cups plain white (all-purpose) flour, pinch of salt and 15 ml/1 tbsp olive oil to 2 eggs (size 2) for 3–4 servings, depending on the required size of portion.

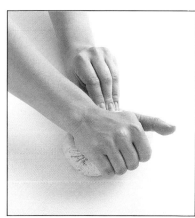

1 Sift the flour and salt on to a clean work surface and make a well in the centre with your fist.

2 Pour the beaten eggs and oil into the well. Gradually mix the eggs into the flour with the fingers of one hand.

3 Knead the pasta until smooth, wrap and allow to rest for at least 30 minutes before attempting to roll out. The pasta will be much more elastic after resting.

Using a Food Processor

1 Sift the flour into the bowl and add a pinch of salt.

2 Pour in the beaten eggs and oil and any chosen flavouring, and process until the dough begins to come together.

3 Tip out the dough and knead until smooth. Wrap and rest for 30 minutes. Use as required.

Using a Pasta Machine

1 Feed the rested dough several times through the highest setting first, then reducing the settings until the required thickness is achieved.

2 A special cutter will produce fettuccine or tagliatelle.

3 A narrower cutter will produce spaghetti or tagliarini.

COOK'S TIP
These are only guidelines: depending on the air humidity, the type of flour and so on, you may have to add more flour. The dough must not be too soft – it should be quite hard to knead. Too much extra flour will make the pasta tough and taste floury!

WATER NEEDED TO COOK PASTA
4 litres/7 pints/4½ quarts water plus 45 ml/3 tbsp salt for every 300–450 g/11 oz–1 lb/3–4 cups dried pasta or 300–450 g/11 oz–1 lb fresh pasta. This will prevent the pasta from sticking.

FLAVOURED PASTA
Tomato Pasta
Add 30 ml/2 tbsp tomato paste to the flour. Use about 1½ eggs.

Beetroot Pasta
Add 30 ml/2 tbsp grated cooked beetroot to the flour. Use about 1½ eggs.

Saffron Pasta
Soak a sachet of powdered saffron in 30 ml/2 tbsp hot water for 15 minutes. Use 1½ eggs and whisk the saffron water into them.

Herb Pasta
Add 45 ml/3 tbsp chopped fresh herbs to the flour.

Wholemeal Pasta
Use 150 g/5 oz/1¼ cups wholemeal flour sifted with 25 g/1 oz/¼ cup plain white (all-purpose) flour and 2 eggs.

Macaroni

Macaroni is the generic name for any hollow pasta. This method is for making garganelle.

1 Cut squares of pasta dough using a sharp knife on a floured surface.

2 Wrap the squares around a pencil or chopstick on the diagonal to form tubes. Slip off and allow to dry slightly.

SPINACH PASTA

Use 150 g/5 oz frozen leaf spinach, cooked and squeezed of moisture, pinch of salt, 2 eggs, about 200 g/ 7 oz 1¾ cups plain white (all-purpose) flour, or a little more if the pasta is sticky. Proceed as for Basic Pasta Dough, but liquidize the spinach with the eggs to give a fine texture.

Tagliatelle

Tagliatelle can also be made with a pasta machine, but it is fairly straightforward to make it by hand.

1 Roll up the floured pasta dough like a Swiss (jelly) roll.

2 Cut the roll into thin slices with a sharp knife. Immediately unravel the slices to reveal the pasta ribbons. To make tagliarini, cut the slices 3 mm/⅛ in thick.

3 To make pappardelle, using a serrated pastry wheel, cut out wide ribbons from the rolled pasta dough.

Tortellini

Tortellini or 'little twists' can be made with meat or vegetarian fillings and served with sauce or in a soup.

1 Using a round biscuit (cookie) cutter, stamp out rounds of pasta.

2 Pipe or spoon the chosen filling into the middle of each round.

3 Brush the edges with beaten egg and fold the round into a crescent shape, excluding all the air. Bend the 2 corners round to meet each other and press well to seal. Repeat with the remaining dough. Leave to dry on a floured tea (dish) towel for 30 minutes before cooking.

SPINACH, RICOTTA AND PARMESAN FILLING FOR STUFFED PASTA
Serves 4–6

450 g/1 lb frozen spinach, thawed and squeezed dry
½ tsp freshly grated nutmeg
5 ml/1 tsp salt
freshly ground black pepper
175 g/6 oz/¾ cup fresh ricotta or curd (cottage) cheese
25 g/1 oz/¼ cup freshly grated Parmesan cheese

Place all the ingredients in a food processor and process until smooth. Use as required.

Ravioli

Although ravioli can be bought ready made, the very best is made at home. Serve with sauce or in a soup.

1 Cut the dough in half and wrap one portion in clear film (plastic wrap). Roll out the pasta thinly to a rectangle on a lightly floured surface. Cover with a clean damp tea (dish) towel and repeat with the remaining pasta. Pipe small mounds (about 5 ml/1 tsp) of filling in even rows, spacing them at 4 cm/1 ½ in intervals, across one piece of the dough. Brush the spaces between the filling with egg.

2 Using a rolling pin, lift the remaining sheet of pasta over the dough with the filling. Press down firmly between the pockets of filling, pushing out any air.

3 Cut into squares with a serrated ravioli cutter or sharp knife. Transfer to a floured tea towel and rest for 1 hour before cooking.

Minestrone

A classic substantial winter soup originally from Milan, but found in various versions around the Mediterranean coasts of Italy and France. Cut the vegetables as roughly or as small as you like. Add freshly grated Parmesan cheese just before serving.

Serves 6–8

INGREDIENTS

225 g/8 oz/2 cups dried haricot
  (navy) beans
30 ml/2 tbsp olive oil
50 g/2 oz smoked streaky bacon,
  diced
2 large onions, sliced
2 garlic cloves, crushed
2 medium carrots, diced
3 celery sticks, sliced
400 g/14 oz canned chopped
  tomatoes
2.25 litres/4 pints/10 cups beef stock
350 g/12 oz potatoes, diced
175 g/6 oz/1½ cups small pasta
  shapes (macaroni, stars, shells, etc)
225 g/8 oz green cabbage, thinly
  sliced
175 g/6 oz fine green beans, sliced
100 g/4 oz/¾ cup frozen peas
45 ml/3 tbsp chopped fresh parsley
salt and pepper
freshly grated Parmesan cheese,
  to serve

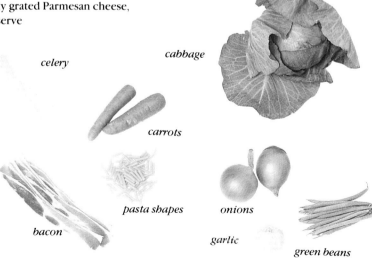

celery

cabbage

carrots

pasta shapes

onions

bacon

garlic

green beans

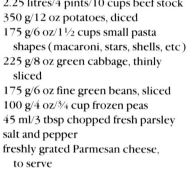

1 Cover the beans with cold water and leave to soak overnight.

2 Heat the oil in a large saucepan and add the bacon, onions and garlic. Cover and cook gently for 5 minutes, stirring occasionally, until soft.

3 Add the carrots and celery and cook for 2–3 minutes until softening.

4 Drain the beans and add to the pan with the tomatoes and stock. Cover and simmer for 2–2½ hours, until the beans are tender.

5 Add the potatoes 30 minutes before the soup is finished.

VARIATION

To make Soupe au Pistou from the South of France, stir in a basil, garlic and pine nut sauce (pesto or pistou) just before serving.

6 Add the pasta, cabbage, beans, peas and parsley 15 minutes before the soup is ready. Season to taste and serve with a bowl of freshly grated Parmesan cheese.

Italian Bean and Pasta Soup

A thick and hearty soup which, followed by bread and cheese, makes a substantial lunch.

Serves 6

INGREDIENTS

175 g/6 oz/1½ cups dried haricot
  (navy) beans, soaked overnight in
  cold water
1.75 litres/3 pints/7½ cups chicken
  stock or water
100 g/4 oz/1 cup medium pasta shells
60 ml/4 tbsp olive oil, plus extra to
  serve
2 garlic cloves, crushed
60 ml/4 tbsp chopped fresh parsley
salt and pepper

parsley

haricot (navy) beans

pasta shells

garlic

1 Drain the beans and place in a large saucepan with the stock or water. Simmer, half-covered, for 2–2½ hours or until tender.

2 Liquidize half the beans and a little of their cooking liquid, then stir into the remaining beans in the pan.

3 Add the pasta and simmer gently for 15 minutes until tender. (Add extra water or stock if the soup seems too thick.)

4 Heat the oil in a small pan and fry the garlic until golden. Stir into the soup with the parsley and season well with salt and pepper. Ladle into individual bowls and drizzle each with a little extra olive oil.

Courgette Soup with Small Pasta Shells

A pretty, fresh-tasting soup which could be made using cucumber instead of courgettes (zucchini).

Serves 4–6

INGREDIENTS
60 ml/4 tbsp olive or sunflower oil
2 medium onions, finely chopped
1.5 litres/2½ pints/6¼ cups chicken
  stock
900 g/2 lb courgettes (zucchini)
100 g/4 oz/1 cup small soup pasta
fresh lemon juice
salt and pepper
30 ml/2 tbsp chopped fresh chervil
soured cream, to serve

courgettes (zucchini)

onion

soup pasta

chervil

1 Heat the oil in a large saucepan and add the onions. Cover and cook gently for about 20 minutes until very soft but not coloured, stirring occasionally.

2 Add the stock and bring to the boil.

3 Meanwhile grate the courgettes and stir into the boiling stock with the pasta. Turn down the heat and simmer for 15 minutes until the pasta is tender. Season to taste with lemon juice, salt and pepper.

4 Stir in the chervil and add a swirl of soured cream before serving.

COOK'S TIP
If no fresh stock is available, instead of using a stock cube, use canned chicken or beef consommé instead.

Provençal Fish Soup with Pasta

This colourful soup has all the flavours of the Mediterranean.
Serve it as a main course for a deliciously filling lunch.

Serves 4

INGREDIENTS
30 ml/2 tbsp olive oil
1 medium onion, sliced
1 garlic clove, crushed
1 leek, sliced
225 g/8 oz canned chopped tomatoes
pinch of Mediterranean herbs
¼ tsp saffron threads (optional)
100 g/4 oz/1 cup small pasta
salt and pepper
about 8 live mussels
450 g/1 lb filleted and skinned white
    fish (cod, plaice, monkfish)

ROUILLE
2 garlic cloves, crushed
1 canned pimento, drained and
    chopped
15 ml/1 tbsp fresh white breadcrumbs
60 ml/4 tbsp mayonnaise
toasted French bread, to serve

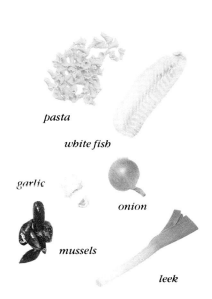

pasta

white fish

garlic

onion

mussels

leek

1 Heat the oil in a large saucepan and add the onion, garlic and leek. Cover and cook gently for 5 minutes, stirring occasionally until soft.

2 Pour in 1 litre/1¾ pints/4½ cups water, the tomatoes, herbs, saffron and pasta. Season with salt and pepper and cook for 15–20 minutes.

3 Scrub the mussels and pull off the 'beards'. Discard any that will not close when sharply tapped: they are almost certainly dead.

4 Cut the fish into bite-sized chunks and add to the soup, placing the mussels on top. Simmer with the lid on for 5–10 minutes until the mussels open and the fish is just cooked. (If any mussels fail to open, discard them.)

5 To make the *rouille*, pound the garlic, canned pimento and breadcrumbs together in a pestle and mortar (or in a food processor). Stir in the mayonnaise and season well.

6 Spread the toasted French bread with the *rouille* and serve with the soup.

Pasta with Roasted Pepper and Tomato Sauce

Add other vegetables such as French beans or courgettes (zucchini) or even chick peas (garbanzos) to make this sauce more substantial.

Serves 4

INGREDIENTS
2 medium red (bell) peppers
2 medium yellow (bell) peppers
45 ml/3 tbsp olive oil
1 medium onion, sliced
2 garlic cloves, crushed
½ tsp mild chilli powder
400 g/14 oz canned chopped plum
    tomatoes
salt and pepper
450 g/1 lb/4 cups dried pasta shells or
    spirals
freshly grated Parmesan cheese, to
    serve

peppers

pasta shells

onion

garlic

1 Pre-heat the oven to 200°C/400°F/ gas mark 6. Place the peppers on a baking sheet or in a roasting tin (roasting pan) and bake for about 20 minutes or until beginning to char. Alternatively grill (broil) the peppers, turning frequently.

2 Rub the skins off the peppers under cold water. Halve, remove the seeds and roughly chop the flesh.

3 Heat the oil in a medium saucepan and add the onion and garlic. Cook gently for 5 minutes until soft and golden.

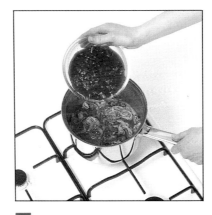

4 Stir in the chilli powder, cook for 2 minutes, then add the tomatoes and peppers. Bring to the boil and simmer for 10–15 minutes until slightly thickened and reduced. Season to taste.

5 Cook the pasta in plenty of boiling salted water according to the manufacturer's instructions. Drain well and toss with the sauce. Serve piping hot with lots of Parmesan cheese.

Spaghetti with Fresh Tomato Sauce

The heat from the pasta will release the delicious flavours of this sauce. Only use the really red and soft tomatoes – large ripe beefsteak or Marmande tomatoes are ideal. Don't be tempted to use small hard tomatoes: they have very little flavour.

Serves 4

INGREDIENTS
4 large ripe tomatoes
2 garlic cloves, finely chopped
60 ml/4 tbsp chopped fresh herbs
    such as basil, marjoram, oregano or
    parsley
150 ml/5 fl oz/⅔ cup olive oil
salt and pepper
450 g/1 lb spaghetti

olive oil

garlic

spaghetti

tomato

VARIATION

Mix 100 g/4 oz/¾ cup stoned (pitted) and chopped black Greek-style olives into the sauce just before serving.

1 Skin the tomatoes by placing in boiling water for 1 minute – no longer or they will become mushy.

2 Lift out with a perforated spoon and plunge into a bowl of cold water. Peel off the skins, then dry the tomatoes on kitchen paper.

3 Halve the tomatoes and squeeze out the seeds. Chop into 6 mm/¼ in cubes and mix with the garlic, herbs, olive oil and seasoning in a non-metallic bowl. Cover and allow the flavours to mellow for at least 30 minutes.

4 Cook the pasta in plenty of boiling salted water.

5 Drain the pasta and mix with the sauce. Cover with a lid and leave for 2–3 minutes, toss again and serve immediately.

Rigatoni with GarlicCrumbs

A hot and spicy dish – halve the quantity of chilli if you like a milder flavour. The bacon is an addition for meat-eaters; leave it out or replace it with sliced mushrooms, if you prefer.

Serves 4–6

INGREDIENTS
45 ml/3 tbsp olive oil
2 shallots, chopped
8 rashers (slices) streaky bacon,
    chopped (optional)
10 ml/2 tsp crushed dried chillies
400 g/14 oz canned chopped
    tomatoes with garlic and herbs
6 slices white bread
100 g/4 oz/½ cup butter
2 garlic cloves, chopped
450 g/1 lb/4 cups rigatoni
salt and pepper

olive oil

garlic

rigatoni

shallots

dried chillies

1 Heat the oil in a medium saucepan and fry the shallots and bacon gently for 6–8 minutes until golden. Add the dried chillies and chopped tomatoes, half-cover and simmer for 20 minutes.

2 Meanwhile cut the crusts off the bread and discard them. Reduce the bread to crumbs in a food processor.

3 Heat the butter in a frying pan (skillet), add the garlic and breadcrumbs and stir-fry until golden and crisp. (Don't let the crumbs catch and burn or the dish will be ruined!)

4 Cook the pasta in boiling salted water according to the manufacturer's instructions. Drain well.

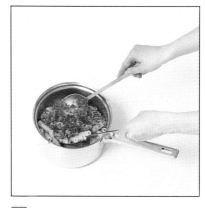

5 Toss the pasta with the tomato sauce and divide between 4 serving bowls.

6 Sprinkle with the crumbs and serve immediately.

Pasta Shells with Tomatoes and Rocket

This pretty-coloured pasta dish relies for its success on a salad green called rocket (arugula). Available in large supermarkets, it is a leaf easily grown in the garden or a window box and tastes slightly peppery.

Serves 4

INGREDIENTS
450 g/1 lb/4 cups pasta shells
salt and pepper
450 g/1 lb ripe cherry tomatoes
45 ml/3 tbsp olive oil
Parmesan cheese, to serve
75 g/3 oz fresh rocket

olive oil

pasta shells

cherry tomatoes

Parmesan cheese

rocket (arugula)

1 Cook the pasta in plenty of boiling salted water according to the manufacturer's instructions. Drain well.

2 Halve the tomatoes. Trim, wash and dry the rocket (arugula).

3 Heat the oil in a large saucepan, add the tomatoes and cook for barely 1 minute. The tomatoes should only just heat through and not disintegrate.

4 Shave the Parmesan cheese using a rotary vegetable peeler.

5 Add the pasta, then the rocket. Carefully stir to mix and heat through. Season well with salt and freshly ground black pepper. Serve immediately with plenty of shaved Parmesan cheese.

Green Pasta with Avocado Sauce

This is an unusual sauce with a pale green colour, studded with red tomato. It has a luxurious velvety texture. The sauce is rather rich, so you don't need too much of it.

Serves 6

INGREDIENTS
3 ripe tomatoes
2 large ripe avocados
25 g/1 oz/2 tbsp butter, plus extra for
   tossing the pasta
1 garlic clove, crushed
450 ml/12 fl oz/1½ cups double
   (heavy) cream
salt and pepper
dash of Tabasco sauce
450 g/1 lb green tagliatelle
freshly grated Parmesan cheese
60 ml/4 tbsp soured cream

tagliatelle

tomatoes

avocado

garlic

1 Halve the tomatoes and remove the cores. Squeeze out the seeds and cut the tomatoes into dice. Set aside.

2 Halve the avocados, take out the stones (pits) and peel. Roughly chop up the flesh.

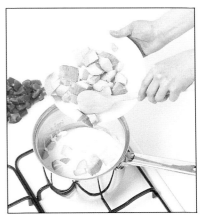

3 Melt the butter in a saucepan and add the garlic. Cook for 1 minute, then add the cream and chopped avocados. Raise the heat, stirring constantly to break up the avocados.

4 Add the diced tomatoes and season to taste with salt, pepper and a little Tabasco sauce. Keep warm.

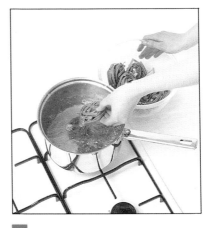

5 Cook the pasta in plenty of boiling salted water according to the manufacturer's instructions. Drain well and toss with a knob of butter.

6 Divide the pasta between 4 warmed bowls and spoon over the sauce. Sprinkle with grated Parmesan and top with a spoonful of soured cream.

Spaghetti with Creamy Mussel and Saffron Sauce

In this recipe the pasta is tossed with a delicious pale yellow mussel sauce, streaked with yellow threads of saffron. Powdered saffron will do just as well, but don't use turmeric – the flavour will be too strong.

Serves 4

INGREDIENTS

900 g/2 lb live mussels
150 ml/5 fl oz/⅔ cup dry white wine
2 shallots, finely chopped
25 g/1 oz/2 tbsp butter
2 garlic cloves, crushed
10 ml/2 tsp cornflour (cornstarch)
300 ml/10 fl oz/1¼ cups double (heavy) cream
pinch of saffron threads
salt and pepper
juice of ½ lemon
1 egg yolk
450 g/1 lb spaghetti
chopped fresh parsley, to garnish

spaghetti   *parsley*

mussels

garlic

shallots

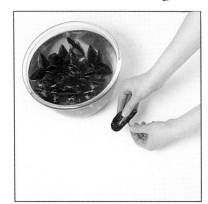

1 Scrub the mussels and rinse well. Pull off any 'beards' and leave the shellfish to soak in cold water for 30 minutes. Tap each mussel sharply after this time. Any that do not close straight away are dead and should be thrown away.

2 Drain the mussels and place in a large saucepan. Add the wine and shallots, cover and cook (shaking frequently) over a high heat for 5–10 minutes until the mussels are open. If some do not open at this stage, throw them out.

3 Pass through a sieve (strainer), reserving the liquid. Remove most of the mussels from their shells. Reserve some in the shell to use as a garnish. Boil the reserved liquid rapidly in a medium saucepan until reduced by half.

4 Melt the butter in another saucepan, add the garlic and cook until golden. Stir in the cornflour (cornstarch) and gradually stir in the cooking liquid and the cream. Add the saffron and seasoning and simmer until slightly thickened.

5 Stir in lemon juice to taste, then the egg yolk and mussels. Keep warm, but do not boil.

6 Cook the pasta in plenty of boiling salted water according to the manufacturer's instructions. Drain well. Toss the mussels with the spaghetti, garnish with the reserved mussels in their shells and sprinkle with the chopped parsley. Serve immediately with lots of crusty bread.

Pasta Spirals with Pepperoni and Tomato Sauce

A warming supper dish, perfect for cold winter nights. All types of sausage are suitable, but if using raw sausages, make sure that they go in with the onion to cook thoroughly.

Serves 4

INGREDIENTS
1 medium onion
1 red (bell) pepper
1 green (bell) pepper
30 ml/2 tbsp olive oil, plus extra for
  tossing the pasta
800 g/1¾ lb canned chopped
  tomatoes
30 ml/2 tbsp tomato purée (paste)
10 ml/2 tsp paprika
175 g/6 oz pepperoni or chorizo
  (spicy sausage)
45 ml/3 tbsp chopped fresh parsley
salt and pepper
450 g/1 lb/4 cups pasta spirals
  (fusilli)

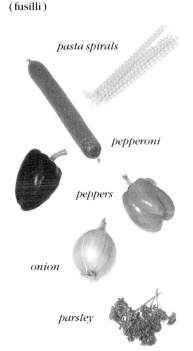

pasta spirals

pepperoni

peppers

onion

parsley

1 Chop the onion. Halve and seed the peppers, removing the cores, then cut the flesh into dice.

2 Heat the oil in a medium saucepan, add the onion and cook for 2–3 minutes until beginning to colour. Stir in the peppers, tomatoes, tomato purée (paste) and paprika, bring to the boil and simmer uncovered for 15–20 minutes until reduced and thickened.

3 Slice the pepperoni and stir into the sauce with 30 ml/2 tbsp chopped parsley. Season to taste.

4 While the sauce is simmering, cook the pasta in plenty of boiling salted water according to the manufacturer's instructions. Drain well. Toss the pasta with the remaining parsley in a little extra olive oil. Divide between warmed bowls and top with the sauce.

Spaghetti with Tomato and Clam Sauce

Small sweet clams make this a delicately succulent sauce. Cockles would make a good substitute, or even mussels. Don't be tempted to use seafood pickled in vinegar – the result will be inedible!

Serves 4

INGREDIENTS
900 g/2 lb live small clams, or 2 ×
    400 g/14 oz cans clams in brine,
    drained
90 ml/6 tbsp olive oil
2 garlic cloves, crushed
600 g/1 lb 5 oz canned chopped
    tomatoes
45 ml/3 tbsp chopped fresh parsley
salt and pepper
450 g/1 lb spaghetti

olive oil   *spaghetti*

parsley

garlic

clams

1 If using live clams, place them in a bowl of cold water and rinse several times to remove any grit or sand. Drain.

2 Heat the oil in a saucepan and add the clams. Stir over a high heat until the clams open. Throw away any that do not open. Transfer the clams to a bowl with a perforated spoon.

3 Reduce the clam juice left in the pan to almost nothing by boiling fast; this will also concentrate the flavour. Add the garlic and fry until golden. Pour in the tomatoes, bring to the boil and cook for 3–4 minutes until reduced. Stir in the clam mixture or canned clams and half the parsley and heat through. Season.

4 Cook the pasta in plenty of boiling salted water according to the manufacturer's instructions. Drain well and turn into a warm serving dish. Pour over the sauce and sprinkle with the remaining parsley.

Pasta with Tuna, Capers and Anchovies

This piquant sauce could be made without the addition of tomatoes – just heat the oil, add the other ingredients and heat through gently before tossing with the pasta.

Serves 4

INGREDIENTS
400 g/14 oz canned tuna fish in oil
30 ml/2 tbsp olive oil
2 garlic cloves, crushed
800 g/1¾ lb canned chopped
    tomatoes
6 canned anchovy fillets, drained
30 ml/2 tbsp capers in vinegar,
    drained
30 ml/2 tbsp chopped fresh basil
salt and pepper
450 g/1 lb/4 cups rigatoni, penne or
    garganelle
sprigs fresh basil, to garnish

olive oil

rigatoni *tuna fish*

basil

anchovy fillets

capers

garlic

1 Drain the oil from the tuna into a saucepan, add the olive oil and heat gently until it stops 'spitting'.

2 Add the garlic and fry until golden. Stir in the tomatoes and simmer for 25 minutes until thickened.

3 Flake the tuna and cut the anchovies in half. Stir into the sauce with the capers and chopped basil. Season well.

4 Cook the pasta in plenty of boiling salted water according to the manufacturer's instructions. Drain well and toss with the sauce. Garnish with fresh basil sprigs.

Pasta Bows with Smoked Salmon and Dill

In Italy, pasta cooked with smoked salmon is becoming very fashionable. This is a quick and luxurious sauce.

Serves 4

INGREDIENTS
6 spring onions (scallions), sliced
50 g/2 oz/4 tbsp butter
90 ml/6 tbsp dry white wine or
    vermouth
450 ml/15 fl oz/2 cups double (heavy)
    cream
salt and pepper
freshly grated nutmeg
225 g/8 oz smoked salmon
30 ml/2 tbsp chopped fresh dill or
    15 ml/1 tbsp dried dillweed
freshly squeezed lemon juice
450 g/1 lb/4 cups pasta bows (farfalle)

pasta bows

lemon

spring onions (scallions)

smoked salmon

nutmeg

dill

I Slice the spring onions (scallions) finely. Melt the butter in a saucepan and fry the spring onions for 1 minute until softened.

2 Add the wine and boil hard to reduce to about 30 ml/2 tbsp. Stir in the cream and add salt, pepper and nutmeg to taste. Bring to the boil and simmer for 2–3 minutes until slightly thickened.

3 Cut the smoked salmon into 2.5 cm/ 1 in squares and stir into the sauce with the dill. Taste and add a little lemon juice. Keep warm.

4 Cook the pasta in plenty of boiling salted water according to the manufacturer's instructions. Drain well. Toss the pasta with the sauce and serve immediately.

Prawns with Tagliatelle and Pesto in Packets

A quick and impressive dish, easy to prepare in advance and cook at the last minute. When the packets are opened, the filling smells wonderful.

Serves 4

INGREDIENTS

750 g/1½ lb medium raw prawns
    (shrimp), shells on
450 g/1 lb tagliatelle or similar pasta
salt and pepper
150 ml/5 fl oz/⅔ cup fresh pesto
    sauce or ready-made equivalent
20 ml/4 tsp olive oil
1 garlic clove, crushed
100 ml/4 fl oz/½ cup dry white wine

olive oil

tagliatelle

pesto sauce

prawns (shrimp)

garlic

1 Pre-heat the oven to 200°C/400°F/ gas mark 6. Twist the heads off the prawns (shrimp) and discard.

2 Cook the tagliatelle in plenty of boiling salted water for 2 minutes only, then drain. Mix with half the pesto.

3 Cut 4 × 30 cm/12 in squares of greaseproof (baking) paper and place 5 ml/1 tsp olive oil in the centre of each. Pile equal amounts of pasta in the middle of each square.

4 Top with equal amounts of prawns and spoon the remaining pesto mixed with the crushed garlic over the prawns. Season with black pepper and sprinkle each serving with 30 ml/2 tbsp wine.

5 Brush the edges of the paper lightly with water and bring them loosely up around the filling, twisting tightly to enclose. (The parcels should look like money bags.)

6 Place the parcels on a baking sheet. Bake in the oven for 10–15 minutes. Serve immediately, allowing each person to open his/her own packet.

Rigatoni with Spicy Sausage and Tomato Sauce

This is really a cheat's Bolognese sauce using the wonderful fresh spicy sausages sold in every Italian delicatessen.

Serves 4

INGREDIENTS

450 g/1 lb fresh spicy Italian sausage
30 ml/2 tbsp olive oil
1 medium onion, chopped
450 ml/15 fl oz/2 cups passata
  (strained crushed tomatoes)
150 ml/5 fl oz/⅔ cup dry red wine
6 sun-dried tomatoes in oil, drained
salt and pepper
450 g/1 lb/4 cups rigatoni or similar
  pasta
freshly grated Parmesan cheese, to
  serve

rigatoni

Italian sausage

Parmesan cheese

onion

sun-dried tomatoes

1 Squeeze the sausages out of their skins into a bowl and break up the meat.

2 Heat the oil in a medium saucepan and add the onion. Cook for 5 minutes until soft and golden. Stir in the sausagemeat, browning it all over and breaking up the lumps with a wooden spoon. Pour in the passata and the wine. Bring to the boil.

3 Slice the sun-dried tomatoes and add to the sauce. Simmer for 3 minutes until reduced, stirring occasionally. Season.

4 Cook the pasta in plenty of boiling salted water according to the manufacturer's instructions. Drain well and top with the sauce. Serve with grated Parmesan cheese.

Pasta with Fresh Tomato and Smoky Bacon Sauce

A wonderful sauce to prepare in mid-summer when the tomatoes are ripe and sweet.

Serves 4

INGREDIENTS
900 g/2 lb ripe tomatoes
6 rashers (slices) smoked streaky
    bacon
50 g/2 oz/4 tbsp butter
1 medium onion, chopped
salt and pepper
15 ml/1 tbsp chopped fresh oregano
    or 5 ml/1 tsp dried oregano
450 g/1 lb/4 cups pasta, any variety
freshly grated Parmesan cheese, to
    serve

pasta

oregano

tomatoes

onion

bacon

Parmesan cheese

1 Plunge the tomatoes into boiling water for 1 minute, then into cold water to stop them from becoming mushy. Slip off the skins. Halve the tomatoes, remove the seeds and cores and roughly chop the flesh.

2 Remove the rind from the bacon and roughly chop.

3 Melt the butter in a saucepan and add the bacon. Fry until lightly brown, then add the onion and cook gently for 5 minutes until softened. Add the tomatoes, salt, pepper and oregano. Simmer gently for 10 minutes.

4 Cook the pasta in plenty of boiling salted water according to the manufacturer's instructions. Drain well and toss with the sauce. Serve with grated Parmesan cheese.

Pasta with Prawns and Feta Cheese

This dish combines the richness of fresh prawns (shrimp) with the tartness of feta cheese. Goat's cheese could also be used.

Serves 4

INGREDIENTS
450 g/1 lb medium raw prawns
   (shrimp)
6 spring onions (scallions)
50 g/2 oz/4 tbsp butter
225 g/8 oz feta cheese
small bunch fresh chives
450 g/1 lb/4 cups penne, garganelle or
   rigatoni
salt and pepper

penne

spring onions (scallions)

feta

chives

prawns (shrimp)

1 Remove the heads from the prawns (shrimp) by twisting and pulling off. Peel the prawns and discard the shells. Chop the spring onions (scallions).

2 Melt the butter in a frying pan (skillet) and stir in the prawns. When they turn pink, add the spring onions and cook gently for 1 minute.

3 Cut the feta into 1 cm/½ in cubes.

4 Stir the feta cheese into the prawn mixture and season with black pepper.

5 Cut the chives into 2.5 cm/1 in lengths and stir half into the prawns.

6 Cook the pasta in plenty of boiling salted water according to the manufacturer's instructions. Drain well, pile into a warmed serving dish and top with the sauce. Scatter with the remaining chives and serve.

Tagliatelle with Prosciutto and Parmesan

A really simple dish, prepared in minutes from the best ingredients.

Serves 4

INGREDIENTS
100 g/4 oz prosciutto
450 g/1 lb tagliatelle
salt and pepper
75 g/3 oz/6 tbsp butter
50 g/2 oz/½ cup freshly grated
   Parmesan cheese
few fresh sage leaves, to garnish

tagliatelle

sage

prosciutto

Parmesan cheese

1 Cut the prosciutto into strips of the same width as the tagliatelle. Cook the pasta in plenty of boiling salted water according to manufacturer's instructions.

2 Meanwhile melt the butter gently in a saucepan, stir in the prosciutto strips and heat through, but do not fry.

3 Drain the tagliatelle well and pile into a warm serving dish.

4 Sprinkle over all the Parmesan cheese and pour over the buttery prosciutto. Season well with black pepper and garnish with the sage leaves.

Pasta with Spinach and Anchovy Sauce

Deliciously earthy, this would make a good starter or light supper dish. Add some sultanas (golden raisins) to ring the changes!

Serves 4

INGREDIENTS

900 g/2 lb fresh spinach or 550 g/
  1¼ lb frozen leaf spinach, thawed
450 g/1 lb/4 cups angel hair pasta
salt
60 ml/4 tbsp olive oil
45 ml/3 tbsp pine nuts
2 garlic cloves, crushed
6 canned anchovy fillets or whole
  salted anchovies, drained and
  chopped
butter, for tossing the pasta

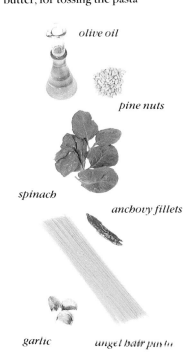

olive oil

pine nuts

spinach

anchovy fillets

garlic   *angel hair pasta*

1 Wash the spinach well and remove the tough stalks. Drain thoroughly. Place in a large saucepan with only the water that still clings to the leaves. Cover with a lid and cook over a high heat, shaking the pan occasionally, until the spinach is just wilted and still bright green. Drain.

2 Cook the pasta in plenty of boiling salted water according to the manufacturer's instructions.

3 Heat the oil in a saucepan and fry the pine nuts until golden. Remove with a perforated spoon. Add the garlic to the oil in the pan and fry until golden. Add the anchovies.

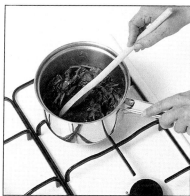

4 Stir in the spinach and cook for 2–3 minutes or until heated through. Stir in the pine nuts. Drain the pasta, toss in a little butter and turn into a warmed serving bowl. Top with the sauce and fork through roughly.

Lasagne al Forno

The classic version of this dish is pasta layered with meat sauce and creamy béchamel sauce. You could vary it by using mozzarella cheese instead of the béchamel sauce, or by mixing ricotta cheese, Parmesan and herbs together instead of the traditional meat sauce.

Serves 4–6

INGREDIENTS
about 12 sheets dried lasagne
1 recipe Bolognese Sauce
about 50 g/2 oz/½ cup freshly grated
    Parmesan cheese
tomato slices and parsley sprig, to
    garnish

BÉCHAMEL SAUCE
850 ml/1½ pints/3¾ cups milk
sliced onion, carrot, celery
few whole peppercorns
50 g/2 oz/½ cup butter
75 g/3 oz/⅔ cup plain (all-purpose)
    flour
salt and pepper
freshly grated nutmeg

1 First make the béchamel sauce. Pour the milk into a saucepan and add the vegetables and peppercorns. Bring to boiling point, remove from the heat and leave to infuse for at least 30 minutes.

2 Strain the milk into a jug. Melt the butter in the same saucepan and stir in the flour. Cook, stirring, for 2 minutes.

3 Remove from the heat and add the milk all in one go, whisk well and return to the heat. Bring to the boil, whisking all the time, then simmer for 2–3 minutes, stirring constantly until thickened. Season to taste with salt, pepper and nutmeg.

lasagne

carrot

onion

celery

Parmesan cheese

Bolognese Sauce

4 Pre-heat the oven to 180°C/350°F/ gas mark 4. If necessary, cook the sheets of lasagne in plenty of boiling salted water according to the instructions. Lift out with a perforated spoon and drain on a clean tea (dish) towel. Spoon one-third of the meat sauce into a buttered baking-dish.

5 Cover the meat sauce with 4 sheets of lasagne and spread with one-third of the béchamel sauce. Repeat twice more, finishing with a layer of béchamel sauce covering the whole top.

6 Sprinkle with Parmesan cheese and bake in the oven for about 15 minutes until brown. Serve garnished with tomato slices and a sprig of parsley.

Cannelloni al Forno

A lighter alternative to the usual beef-filled, béchamel-coated version. Fill with ricotta, onion and mushroom for a vegetarian recipe.

Serves 4–6

INGREDIENTS
450 g/1 lb/4 cups skinned and boned
    chicken breast, cooked
225 g/8 oz mushrooms
2 garlic cloves, crushed
30 ml/2 tbsp chopped fresh parsley
15 ml/1 tbsp chopped fresh tarragon
1 egg, beaten
salt and pepper
fresh lemon juice
12–18 cannelloni tubes
1 recipe Napoletana Sauce
50 g/2 oz/½ cup freshly grated
    Parmesan cheese
1 sprig fresh parsley, to garnish

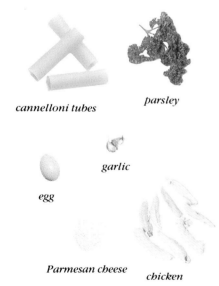

cannelloni tubes   *parsley*

garlic

egg

Parmesan cheese   *chicken*

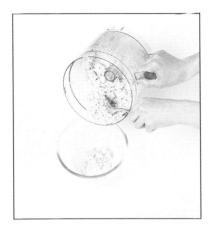

1 Pre-heat the oven to 200°C/400°F/gas mark 6. Place the chicken in a food processor and blend until finely minced (ground). Transfer to a bowl.

2 Place the mushrooms, garlic, parsley and tarragon in the food processor and blend until finely minced.

3 Beat the mushroom mixture into the chicken with the egg, salt and pepper and lemon juice to taste.

4 If necessary, cook the cannelloni in plenty of salted boiling water according to the instructions. Drain well on a clean tea (dish) towel.

5 Place the filling in a piping bag (cone) fitted with a large plain nozzle (tip). Use this to fill each tube of cannelloni.

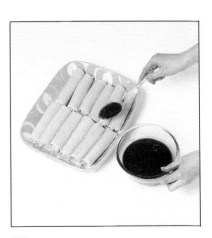

6 Lay the filled cannelloni tightly together in a single layer in a buttered shallow ovenproof dish. Spoon over the tomato sauce and sprinkle with Parmesan cheese. Bake in the oven for 30 minutes or until brown and bubbling. Serve garnished with a sprig of parsley.

Mediterranean Salad with Basil

A type of Salade Niçoise with pasta, conjuring up all the sunny flavours of the Mediterranean.

Serves 4

INGREDIENTS

225 g/8 oz/2 cups chunky pasta shapes
175 g/6 oz fine green beans
2 large ripe tomatoes
50 g/2 oz fresh basil leaves
200 g/7 oz can tuna fish in oil, drained
2 hard-boiled eggs, shelled and sliced
    or quartered
50 g/2 oz can anchovy fillets, drained
capers and black olives

DRESSING

90 ml/6 tbsp extra-virgin olive oil
30 ml/2 tbsp white wine vinegar or
    lemon juice
2 garlic cloves, crushed
2.5 ml/½ tsp Dijon mustard
30 ml/2 tbsp chopped fresh basil
salt and pepper

tomatoes

olive oil

garlic

basil

pasta shapes

egg

anchovy fillets

green beans

tuna fish

1 Whisk all the ingredients for the dressing together and leave to infuse while you make the salad.

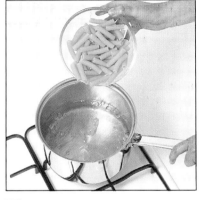

2 Cook the pasta in plenty of boiling salted water according to the manufacturer's instructions. Drain well and cool.

3 Trim the beans and blanch in boiling salted water for 3 minutes. Drain and refresh in cold water.

4 Slice or quarter the tomatoes and arrange on the bottom of a bowl. Moisten with a little dressing and cover with a quarter of the basil leaves. Then cover with the beans. Moisten with a little more dressing and cover with a third of the remaining basil.

5 Cover with the pasta tossed in a little more dressing, half the remaining basil and the roughly flaked tuna.

6 Arrange the eggs on top, then finally scatter over the anchovy fillets, capers and black olives. Pour over the remaining dressing and garnish with the remaining basil. Serve immediately. Don't be tempted to chill this salad – all the flavour will be dulled.

Strawberry Conchiglie Salad with Kirsch and Raspberry Sauce

A divinely decadent dessert laced with liqueur and luscious raspberry sauce.

Serves 4

INGREDIENTS
175 g/6 oz/½ cup pasta shells (conchiglie)
salt
225 g/8 oz fresh or frozen raspberries, thawed if frozen
15–30 ml/1–2 tbsp caster (superfine) sugar
lemon juice
450 g/1 lb small fresh strawberries
flaked almonds
45 ml/3 tbsp kirsch

pasta shells

raspberries

strawberries

almonds

1 Cook the pasta in plenty of boiling salted water according to the manufacturer's instructions. Drain well and cool.

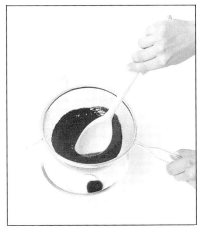

2 Purée the raspberries in a food processor and pass through a sieve (strainer) to remove the seeds.

3 Put the purée in a small saucepan with the sugar and simmer for 5–6 minutes, stirring occasionally. Add lemon juice to taste. Set aside to cool.

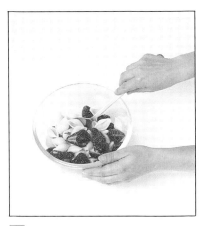

4 Hull the strawberries and halve if necessary. Toss with the pasta and transfer to a serving bowl.

5 Spread the almonds on a baking sheet and toast under the grill (broiler) until golden. Cool.

6 Stir the kirsch into the raspberry sauce and pour over the salad. Scatter with the toasted almonds and serve.

INDEX